Preface

Everyone needs money, right? Everyone needs money since he/she were born to die, he/she need money, right?

The problem is that many people are hard to earn money to meet their daily needs. So how to deal with getting what you want.

Are you unemployed? Are you looking for a job? Are you in trouble for money? Need cash in a hurry? Of course, you do! Right?

If your answer is yes, then you need to read, study, and practice the contents of this book. After that, your fate will change. Ha...7x

Congratulations! Your financial problems can be overcome soon.

Richard Nata is the author of:
1. How to Create Great Articles for SEO in Three Hours.
2. The Best Way To Stop Watching Porn Today.
3. How to Skyrocket 7-8 Figure Income Annually from Blogging.
4. Want More Traffic? 514 Tips to Skyrocket Your Website Traffic and Income Faster.
5. How to Start a Business With China.
6. Why Do Trump and Some Other US Presidents Endorse a New World Order?
7. Knowing Jesus Better - the Real Jesus According to Thousands of Verses and Who is Jesus to you?
8. How to Win a Soul to Jesus Christ.
9. Top Secret of Healthy Life Revealed.
10. Top Secret of Longevity Revealed.
11. Top Secret of Healthy Life and Longevity Revealed.

Thank you for reading my book.
Lord Jesus blesses you.
Amen.
P.S. Thank you for your good review.

Table of Contents

Preface 1
Table of Contents 2
Introduction 3
Kinds of Work Type 6
Determine Your Career Goals 9
Do Not Waste Your Time on Social Media 10
Focus 10
Choose a Job You Love 12
A Full-Time or Part-Time Job 14
A Full-Time Job or Full-Time Freelancer 15
Which Is Better a Full-Time Job or a Full-Time Freelancer? 16
Revenue Target 17
How to Get $5,000 Quickly 22
English as a Second Language (ESL) 24
Be Confident and Immediately Apply for a Job 24
Pray to God 26
Doing a Research 27
Active Income, Passive Income, or Both 28
How to Get Both, Active Income and Passive Income 30
How to Find a Job Faster 31
Create a Great Cover Letter 33
Examples of the Great Cover Letters 36
Create a Great Resume 43
Example of a Great Resume 45
Make Your Cover Letter and Resume Become One Page 48
Use the Power of Words 49
Always Check and Recheck 50
15 Simple Ways to Attract the Company's Attention 51
Create Your Video Profile Then Upload to YouTube 52
Use Your LinkedIn Profile to Attract Boss and/or Headhunter 57
How to Build Your Personal Brand on LinkedIn 58
23 Golden Rules of Seeking a Job 61
Do a Job That No One Else Wants 63
Do Not Take the Job That Enslaving You 63

Internship Jobs 64
401 Professional Jobs That You Can Apply For 65
Test 78
Interview 79
How to Make Your Interviewer Impressed While Interviewing You 81
Lessons Learned: What a Lost Test and/or Interview Really Tells You 83
Salary Strategy 84
Why Didn't You Get a Job There? 85
Tips for Success Facing Your First Day Working 86
19 Golden Rules for Working 88
When It's Time to Move Jobs 89
Never Resign Until You Get a High Salary from the New Job or You Are Fired 90
If You Are Fired, Then Drop Your Ego and Start to Move on Yourself 91
Ready, Set, Go! 92
Conclusion 93

Introduction

Always think digital be global.

Most people dream of living their lives with freedom and passion, doing what they love, then they can finally relax and enjoy life, right?

Before you can get all the dreams above, then you should be able to make your first $5,000, right? To achieve your dream and make your first $5,000 faster. And you will make your own destiny!

If you want to make your first $5,000 (and who doesn't, right?), see if this book is right for you.

This book is the knowledge you've been waiting for a long time. Because this book can show you a **faster**, **easier**, more **stress-free** and enjoyable way to get your first $5,000.

Read, study, and practice to it. Grab your first $5,000. And make something happen to you.

Believe it or not, you can get your first $5,000 faster because it works fine for us.

Do you really understand your passion and motivation to get your first $5,000? If yes, getting your first $5,000 is actually not hard since you know the secret. You will know the tactics to make your first $5,000 faster if you continue to read this book.

If you follow the step by step of this book, then your next step to make your first $5,000 is perfectly clear.

Do not be discouraged if you find this hard to do at first (I know, I did!). Keep practicing and it will become easier day by day.

I believe its your time to make your first $5,000 now. Because this book not only gives theory but gives you guidance to get your first $5,000 faster.

What will you get on this book? Almost everything that makes your first $5,000 faster. So you started to think about how you could make that happen.

Everything you need to know to:
1. You started to think about how you could make your first $5,000 faster.
2. Learn and practice a method for making your first $5,000 with confidence & ease.
3. Looking for a job.
4. Research.
5. You can make your first $5,000 faster.

6. Make a Great Cover Letter.
7. Make a Great Resume.
8. Make a Great video profile.
9. Make many benefits from your social media.
10. Past the interview successfully.
11. And many more.

Remember this!

Making your first $5,000 can be a long process. So you need to put more passion, time, and find the motivation to keep making money. If you can do it, then you've managed to speed up the process to get your first $5,000, right?

> Tony Robbins: "If you want to be successful, find someone who has achieved results you want and copy what they do..."

Richard Nata: Be patient. Success like running a marathon takes a long time. Today is the time for you to change. So just do it and never limit yourself. Then it is not you who pursue success, but success will catch you.

I have been young, and [now] am old; yet have I not seen the righteous forsaken, nor his seed begging bread (Psalms 37:25).

The blessing of the LORD, it maketh rich, and he addeth no sorrow with it (Proverbs 10:22).

Psalms {127:1} Except the LORD build the house, they labour in vain that build it: except the LORD keep the city, the watchman waketh [but] in vain. {127:2} [It is] vain for you to rise up early, to sit up late, to eat the bread of sorrows: [for] so he giveth his beloved sleep.

If you believe the above verses, then you do not have to worry anymore.

You have to work if you want to earn money, right.

If you can earn money without working, then you have turned your life into a beggar, or a robber, or a swindler.

For even when we were with you, this we commanded you, that if any would not work, neither should he eat (2 Thessalonians 3:10).

This book will take your life to a whole new level. For the person who's committed, anything is possible.

Psalms {1:1} Blessed [is] the man that walketh not in the counsel of the ungodly, nor standeth in the way of sinners, nor sitteth in the seat of the scornful. {1:2} But his delight [is] in the law of the LORD; and in his law doth he meditate day and night. {1:3} And he shall be like a tree planted by the rivers of water, that bringeth forth his fruit in his season; his leaf also shall not wither; and whatsoever he doeth shall prosper.

This book does not teach you to Get-rich-quick schemes, but teach you, how to get your first $5,000 faster. After that, you can do it again and again and again. He...7x

So you better figure out how to get your work out there on a bigger scale and make money doing it.

The author believes, if you trust in God, work really hard, and you are kind, amazing things will happen.

Kinds of Work Type

According to Payable.com, a work type is a unit that determines what or how a worker is paid. Payable can accommodate any kind of work or method that you might use to calculate contractor compensation. This can be any common way to pay independent contractors such as Hourly, by the Project, Day Rate, etc. Or something more specific, like Photographs, Deliveries, Articles, or anything another unit of measuring the output of your contractors.

Basically, a work type is divided into:
1. Full-time job. The job takes a lot of your time, you usually work from 9 am to 5 pm. You usually work from Monday to Friday.

Payments are made once a week or month.

Full-time employment often comes with benefits that are not typically offered to part-time, temporary, or flexible workers, such as annual leave, sick leave, and health insurance.

If you can get a high position, then you usually get an annual bonus when the company gets a profit beyond the target set.

2. Part-time job. The job takes the fewer hours per week than a full-time job. You are not required to work from Monday to Friday. So **your working hours are flexible.**

Payments are made once a week/month based on the targets or commissions reached or after the work is done.

Part-time employment does not get annual leave, sick leave, health insurance, and annual bonus.

A part-time worker is also called a freelancer.

Your income as a freelancer depends on how active you are working because the more active you are, the more money you will make.

Besides full-time job and the part-time job, there are some terms you should understand.

1. Contract Job. A contract is an agreement among employee and employer setting out inferred, and implicit terms and conditions.

Employees and employers must stick to a contract until it ends or until the terms are changed.

2. Remote job or Anywhere. A remote job is one that is done away from the office in a remote location. This could be either work did from home or work is done on the road for a job such as a Regional Salesperson.

3. Telework Job or Telecommuting.
A telecommuting job sometimes called teleworking, is one where you trade your commute for a home-based job. Rather than traditional commuting, you are "commuting" by telephone and computer.

Most telecommuting jobs are done from home offices, but they may be part-time or full-time telecommuting jobs, meaning that the company may want you to be in the office for meetings or occasional face-time.

4. Home-Based Job.
This is perhaps the most obvious of all the remote job phrases here. Home-based jobs are those that you do from your home. This is also very similar to a virtual job because, usually, a job that is called home-based will be 100% done from your home without regular trips into the office for meetings and face-time.

Resource: https://www.flexjobs.com/blog/post/what-is-a-remote-job/

Of course, when applying for a job, you should review the job description to make sure that this is the kind of job you want. Therefore, you should do some research before you apply for a job.

Determine Your Career Goals

You must be serious about your career goals because your future is determined by the plan you are creating right now.

The first thing you should do is figure out your career goals. Define success on your own terms and conditions. Then imagining where you want to be in a set number of years.

How much time can you take your position to the next level?
What would be your dream position in the next year?
What would be your dream position in the next five years?
What would be your dream position in the next ten years?
What would be your dream position in the next 25 years?

Remember this! You should set some targets to reach in your career plan.

Then you can write it down on a list.

Write down a list of your main strengths, weaknesses, personality type, skills, abilities, hobbies, and education.

Do not forget to write down, some abilities you want to improve in the future. If you need a degree for your dream role, plan how to get an appropriate degree in the next few years.

You have to believe in yourself. Do what you want. And be cool with it.

Do Not Waste Your Time on Social Media

Remember this!

Do not waste your time on social media.

Note this well. Many people who have spent hours each day to open Facebook, YouTube, Google+, Reddit, Instagram, StumbleUpon, Pinterest, Twitter, etc. And they do not make money at all.

Your time is limited, so don't waste it.

Time is influencing your future. Remember that "time is money" or more precisely to say if you can use your time well, then you will make more money. So, don't spend your valuable time on social media that don't bring you money.

Absolutely, you should make social media to promote your skill, ability, knowledge, experience, and portfolio. But you do not use for things that do not need such as chat, make comments on various posts, and debating any topic.

Steve Jobs said, "Your time is limited, so don't waste it living someone else's life."

Focus

When you are looking for a job, then you have to focus on one or more particular field. To get a job faster, then focus on areas that you like the most. And never turned your attention to other fields.

By focusing, you can quickly find out all the constraints, challenges, and problems while applying for a job. The more focused you are, the faster you can get a job. Stay focused on the creative process. And never lose the vision of your creative process.

The problem is that you often find it difficult to focus, right?

Remember this!
You can focus on the real tactics and strategies. It's mostly about the things you do, not about how you feel.

Some things that distract your focus is:
1. A beep from the telephone, SMS (Short Message Service), or WA (Whatsapp). So turn off your smartphone.
2. Check email, LinkedIn, Facebook, Reddit, and other social media. Specify the time when you open the email, Facebook, Reddit, and other social media. Never open it other than the specified time, except your email. Because you should often check your email to see if there are companies that reply to your job application.
3. TV and Video. So turn off your TV and DVD (Digital Video Disc).
4. Games. So turn off your games.

5. Hang out. Some friends may invite you to hang out. Reject them because you are currently focused on finding a job.

You are not working now. But you can focus on using the time from 9 am to 5 pm to find a job.

Boring? Obviously very boring. But you can get a job faster if you focus on doing this every day until you get a job.

Remember this!

The faster you get a job, the faster you get your first $5,000, right?

So, what are you waiting for?

Be focus and start looking for a job.

Choose a Job You Love

Remember this!

You have to love your job, love what you do, and do what you enjoy.

Don't settle for what other people want you to do, or what you think you should be doing—choose jobs that you are truly passionate about. So you can work on jobs you are obsessed with. This is your perfect job.

Don't listen to those outside voices telling you what your work or career is "supposed" to look like. Do what you love, and focus on achieving what you set out to do. And do whatever you want. This is your perfect job.

Why should you choose the job you love?

Confucius said, "Life is really simple, but we insist on making it complicated. Wherever you go, go with all your heart. It does not matter how slowly you go as long as you do not stop. Our greatest glory is not in never falling, but in rising every time we fall. Choose a job you love and you'll never work a single day in your life."

Steve Jobs said, "Your work is going to fill a large part of your life. And the only way to be truly satisfied is to do what you believe is great work. And the only way to do great work is to love what you do. If you haven't found it yet, keep looking. Don't settle. As with all matters of the heart, you'll know when you find it."

Richard Nata said, "A job that you love makes you know what you should do and do what you know. So, you just follow your passion and **make money living from your passion.** By doing that, the money will come by itself. After that, you can do whatever you want with the money you get. Because money can buy almost anything desired by people for life in this world."

If you do not spend your time to do what you like then you will easily become stressed if you have problems in your work. Right?

Richard Nata said, "Understanding why you really do what you love. If you really love your work, what you do is much more, have more energy, more fun, and more success. Right?"

So, what are you waiting for? You can set a job target you believe in, a job target you love now. This is your perfect job. ☺

After that, you can start applying for work at various companies that open vacancies in accordance with the field you love.

Richard Nata: If you want to succeed faster, then work with all your heart as you work for God.

Philippians {4:13} I can do all things through Christ which strengtheneth me.

Luke {16:10} He that is faithful in that which is least is faithful also in much: and he that is unjust in the least is unjust also in much.

Matthew {10:16} Behold, I send you forth as sheep in the midst of wolves: be ye therefore wise as serpents, and harmless as doves.

Colossians {3:23} And whatsoever ye do, do [it] heartily, as to the Lord, and not unto men;

Philippians {4:19} But my God shall supply all your need according to his riches in glory by Christ Jesus.

Work on the profession you enjoy and obsessed with. Then the job satisfaction and promotion will become your friend. This is your perfect job.

A Full-Time or Part-Time Job

Most people want to work full-time compared to part-time. Because, if they can work full-time, then their salary is paid every month. They get annual leave, sick leave, and health insurance. In addition, they will get various perks, facilities, and bonuses from the company.

Usually, the full-time job salary earned is higher compared to part-time job workers.

Is it true that a full-time job provides a better income than a part-time job? Absolutely right.

Therefore, you should look for a full-time job compared to a part-time job.

Why is that? Because a full-time job has more hours than a part-time job.

The question now is as follows. What if both have the same number of working hours or working hours of a part-time job is more than the working hours of a full-time job? Are the earnings in a full-time job greater than a part-time job?

The answer is not necessarily. The answer depends on your diligence, skill, knowledge, ability, and rate.

Why is that?

Read on this book to get the answer.

A Full-Time Job VS Full-Time Freelancer

If you are working on two or more part-time jobs at once in the same or adjacent time, then you are said to be a full-time freelancer.

Although you work part-time, you can get more income if you are skilled and diligent in finding new jobs.

Examples are as follows.

1. You work as a Staff Writer. Your monthly salary is $3,000. You can complete 3 articles every day. Then you can earn $3,000 a month. For how many articles you make, your salary remains $3,000.

You work as a Freelance Writer. You get paid $50 per article. You can complete 3 articles every day or 90 articles a month. Then you can earn $4,500 a month.

2. You work as a Staff Programmer. Your monthly salary is $5,000. You can complete 2 websites a month. Then you can earn $5,000 a month. For how many websites you make, your salary remains $5,000.

You work as a Freelance Programmer. You get paid $3,000 per website. You can complete 2 websites a month. Then you can earn $6,000 a month.

The question now is why you can get more income if you become a full-time freelancer? The answer is if you work for a company then all the profits earned will belong to the company. And you only get paid with a fixed salary plus a bonus if any. Whereas, if you work as a full-time freelancer, then all the profits will be yours.

So a full-time job or full-time freelancer? Your decision will affect you, on your family, and on your career.

Which Is Better a Full-Time Job or a Full-Time Freelancer?

The answer is not necessarily. The answer depends on your diligence, skill, ability, knowledge, and rate.

The author's suggestion is that if you are just working for the first time, then you should find a job as a full-timer in a company. When working, you should improve your skills, ability, and knowledge so you become an expert in your field of work.

After becoming an expert, you can start looking for freelance work in your field of work. After getting a lot of the repeat clients, then you resign from your job and become a full-time freelancer.

Why is that? Because you will get more income. In addition, you are free to work without having to be managed by a manager and/or boss. Right? Ha...7x

Do you agree with my suggestion? Or you have another strategy. It's up to you. Because this is your life. So you have to decide what you will do to earn money.

You can seek advice from your parents, wife/husband, friends, or neighbors before deciding whether you will be working a full-time job or full-time freelancer.

Revenue Target

The target revenue that the author sets out in this book is $5,000.

Of course, you can create your own target revenue. The more your targeted target, the better.

The example is:

1. Your revenue targeted $10,000.

2. Your revenue targeted $20,000.

You should really understand with your passion and motivation to get your first $5,000.

The target $5,000 is small for some people. But target $5,000 is big for some other people.

2018 Federal and State Minimum Wage Rates per Hour:

1. Alabama: $7.25 (Federal Minimum Wage, no state minimum).
2. Alaska: $9.84 (Annual indexing has begun).
3. Arizona: $10.50 (Raised to $12.00 through Indexed Annual Increases between 1/1/2019 to 1/1/2020).
4. Arkansas: $8.50.
5. California: $11.00 ($11.00 to $15.00 in $1.00 Indexed Annual Increases between 1/1/2019 to 1/1/2022).
6. Colorado: $10.20* ($10.20 to $12.00 in $0.90 Indexed Annual Increases between 1/1/2019 and 1/1/2020).
7. Connecticut: $10.10.
8. Delaware: $8.25.
9. District of Columbia: $12.50 (Increases to $15 with Indexed Annual Increases between 7/1/2018 and 7/1/2020).
10. Florida: $8.25*
11. Georgia: $5.15 if not covered by Federal Regulations otherwise $7.25 (Federal Minimum Wage).
12. Guam: $8.25.
13. Hawaii: $10.10.
14. Idaho: $7.25.
15. Illinois: $8.25.
16. Indiana: $7.25.
17. Iowa: $7.25.
18. Kansas: $7.25.
19. Kentucky: $7.25.
20. Louisiana: $7.25 (Federal Minimum Wage, no state minimum).
21. Maine: $10.00 (11.00 to $12.00 in $1.00 annual Increases between 1/1/2019 to 1/1/2020) (Indexed annual increases will begin on 1/1/2021).
22. Maryland: $10.10.

23. Massachusetts: $11.00 ($3.75 for tipped employees).
24. Michigan: $9.25 (Indexed annual increases will begin on 4/1/2019).
25. Minnesota: Large employers are required to pay workers $9.65/hour and small employers (less than 500k in annual sales) $7.87 (Indexed Annual increases will begin on 1/1/2018).
26. Mississippi: $7.25 (Federal Minimum Wage, no state minimum).
27. Missouri: $7.85.
28. Montana: $8.30 ($4.00 for businesses with gross annual sales of $110,000 or less) (Annual indexing has begun).
29. Nebraska: $9.00.
30. Nevada: $8.25 Nevada's minimum wage is set at $1.00 above the federal minimum wage for firms not providing health insurance.
31. New Hampshire: $7.25 (Federal Minimum Wage).
32. New Jersey: $8.60 (Annual indexing has begun).
33. New Mexico: $7.50.
34. New York: $10.40 ($0.70 Indexed Annual Increases from 12/31/2018 to $12.50 by 12/31/2020. Starting 1/1/2021, the rate will be adjusted annually for inflation until it reaches $15 an hour) - More information on New York minimum wage increases.
35. North Carolina: $7.25.
36. North Dakota: $7.25.
37. Ohio: $8.30 ($7:25 for employers with gross sales of $283,000 or less) (Annual indexing has begun).
38. Oklahoma: $7.25.
39. Oregon: $10.75 (From $10.75 to $13.50 from 7/1/2019 to 7/1/2022).
40. Pennsylvania: $7.25.
41. Puerto Rico: $7.25.
42. Rhode Island: $10.10.

43. South Carolina: $7.25 (Federal Minimum Wage, no state minimum).
44. South Dakota: $8.65 (Annual indexing has begun).
45. Tennessee: $7.25 (Federal Minimum Wage, no state minimum).
46. Texas: $7.25.
47. Utah: $7.25.
48. Vermont: $10.50, Annual indexing begins 1/1/2019.
49. Virgin Islands: $9.50, $10.50, 6/1/18.
50. Virginia: $7.25.
51. Washington: $11.50 (From $12.50 to $13.50 from 1/1/2019-1/1/2020).
52. West Virginia: $8.75.
53. Wisconsin: $7.25.
54. Wyoming: $7.25, $5.15 if federal regulations do not apply.

According to the Economic Policy Institute, 40 localities have adopted minimum wages above their state minimum wage:

Albuquerque, New Mexico; Berkeley, California; Bernalillo County, New Mexico; Birmingham, Alabama; Chicago, Illinois; Cook County, Illinois; Cupertino, California; El Cerrito, California; Emeryville, California; Flagstaff, Arizona; Las Cruces, New Mexico; Los Altos, California; Los Angeles County, California; Los Angeles, California; Malibu, California; Milpitas, California; Montgomery County, Maryland; Mountain View, California; Nassau, Suffolk, and Westchester Counties, New York; New York City, New York; Oakland, California; Palo Alto, California; Pasadena, California; Portland Urban Growth Boundary, Oregon; Portland, Maine; Prince George's County, Maryland; Richmond, California; San Diego, California; San Francisco, California; San Jose, California; San Leandro, California; San Mateo, California; Santa Clara, California; Santa Fe City, New Mexico; Santa Fe County, New Mexico; Santa Monica, California; SeaTac, Washington; Seattle, Washington; Sunnyvale, California; and Tacoma, Washington.

Data source: https://www.thebalancecareers.com/2017-federal-state-minimum-wage-rates-2061043

Top 10 national minimum wages per Hour 2015 in the world:

Australia $9.54.

Luxembourg $9.24.

Belgium $8.57.

Ireland $8.46.

France $8.24.

Netherlands $8.2.

New Zealand $7.55.

Germany $7.19.

Canada $7.18.

United Kingdom $7.06.

Data source: http://money.cnn.com/interactive/economy/top-10-national-minimum-wages-in-the-world/index.html

Working hours: 9 am – 5 pm or 8 hours.

Day hours: Monday – Friday or 5 days.

Week hours: 40 hours.

Bless you, if you live in the countries above because you only need 3 months or more to get your first $5,000.

15 Countries With The Cheapest Labor in 2017:

1. UGANDA - $0.01 per hour or $22 PER YEAR.
2. GEORGIA - $0.24 per hour or $96 PER YEAR.
3. CUBA - $0.05 per hour or $108 PER YEAR.
4. KYRGYZSTAN - $0.09 per hour, gets $14 per month or $181 PER YEAR.
5. BANGLADESH – $0.09 per hour, gets $19 per month or $228 PER YEAR.
6. TANZANIA - $0.1 per hour or $240 PER YEAR.
7. THE GAMBIA - $0.13 per hour or $317 PER YEAR.
8. VENEZUELA - $0.17 per hour or $361 PER YEAR.
9. GUINEA-BISSAU - $0.17 per hour or $372 PER YEAR.
10. MALAWI - $0.17 per hour or $412 PER YEAR.
11. LIBERIA - $0.17 per hour or $435 PER YEAR.
12. THE DEMOCRATIC REPUBLIC OF THE CONGO - $0.2 per hour or $472 PER YEAR.
13. TAJIKISTAN - $0.23 per hour or $487 PER YEAR.
14. GHANA - $0.23 per hour or $488 PER YEAR.
15. MADAGASCAR - $0.23 per hour or $490 PER YEAR.

Data source: https://www.therichest.com/world-money/15-countries-with-the-cheapest-labor/

If you live in the 15 countries above, then you need ten years or more to get your first $5,000.

Do not be too sad. Because this book will teach you how to earn $5,000 faster.

How to Get $5,000 Quickly

Here are some things you should do so you can get $5,000 quickly:

1. Pray to God.
2. Improve your English skills so you can read and write in English.
3. Doing a research.
4. **Start applying for work online.** Because it does not cost you anything, except the cost of using the internet. He...7x
5. Become the members of several job search sites like Indeed, Simple Hired, Upwork, Freelancer, Guru, FlexJobs, etc.
6. If your skills are writing, then you can apply through the websites that provide premium payment likes Problogger, IZEA, ClearVoice, CloudPeeps, Express Writers, etc.
7. Create your video profile then upload to YouTube.
8. Use your LinkedIn profile to attract the boss and/or Headhunter.
9. Building your personnel brand on LinkedIn.
10. Send your "Cover Letters + Resume" as much as possible every day.
11. Never stop sending your "Cover Letters + Resume" even if you've been interviewed. Because you may not be agreed to work there.
12. Never stop sending "Cover Letters + Resume" until you are agreed to work in a company.
13. The most important thing is that you can start working as soon as possible. So do not trouble how much your salary.
14. After you are agreed to work in a company, then increase your skill and ability.
15. Be smart and intelligent.
16. Be the master in your field.
17. Be helpful for your boss.
18. **Building trust.**
19. **Plan your future.**
20. After you work 3-5 years and become an expert in the field, you can move to another company. Or you just try to find a freelance job. If you can get a lot of clients, then you can

resign from the company to start working as a full-time freelancer.

"Stay afraid, but do it anyway. What's important is the action. You don't have to wait to be confident. Just do it and eventually the confidence will follow" – Carrie Fisher.

English as a Second Language (ESL)

Bless you, if English is your native language. You will not have the difficulty in finding work on various international websites.

Conversely, if English is not your native language, then you should be able to speak English first before you look for work on various international websites.

If your English is fluent, then you already have three skills as a translator or interpreter or Video/Audio Transcript.

Remember this!

If you want to make your first $5,000 faster, then think digital, be global.

Look for online jobs that you can do at home.

You can search for remote jobs and/or contract jobs. You can even search for one or more jobs at once.

Be Confident and Immediately Apply for a Job

Many people are afraid to apply for work on various international websites because they think that their English is not good.

In fact, they are afraid of their own. Because who knows and who cares if your English is not good? Right?

To be honest, the English by the author is also mediocre. But the author is always confident to apply for work or make a bid on various international websites.

Why do the author dare to do that? The author dares to do it because the author has several strategies to overcome this problem.

There are four reasons why the author dare to do that:

1. There are many tools that make it easy for us to work. Currently, many softwares or tools translator from English to your language or vice versa. An example is we can use Google to translate online. Of course, Google translate is not accurate, so there are many mistakes when it translates a sentence.
2. The lack of Google translate can be covered with tools that can check for grammar, spelling, and typo errors. So this tool can does proofreading for you. There are many tools that you can use, either free or paid.
3. Besides tools, you can also use the services of someone to do editing and proofreading. You pay according to his expertise. The more expert the more expensive the price of the service you have to pay.

4. You can find a freelancer to do the tasks assigned to you. Of course, you pay for a cheaper price. An example is you get a gig to create two articles for $25 per article. Then you look for a freelancer who wants to work on the gig at a price of $10 per article. If successful, then you earn a profit of $15 per article or $30 per gig.

You can do it too if you know how to overcome your shortcomings in English.

In facts, some famous bloggers in their articles often have errors in grammar, spelling, and typo. So do not ever be afraid to make mistakes in writing. Right? Ha...7x

Pray to God

Always involve God in your plans. Ask God's direction and wisdom!

Pray that God will always intervene so that you can get the job quickly.

Romans {8:28} And we know that all things work together for good to them that love God, to them who are the called according to [his] purpose.

Philippians {4:13} I can do all things through Christ which strengtheneth me.

Philippians {4:19} But my God shall supply all your need according to his riches in glory by Christ Jesus. {4:20} Now unto God and our Father [be] glory for ever and ever. Amen.

If you do not mind, then you can pray to the Lord Jesus. For Jesus is the Lord of the heavens and the earth.

You can see the evidence that Jesus is the creator of the universe and man through my book entitled "Top Secret of Healthy Life and Longevity Revealed."

If you want, then you can pray like this.

Father in the name of Jesus. Today I came to You to ask for Your help. I'm looking for a job to earn $5,000 as soon as possible.

After earning $5,000, I hope You will multiply it so I will not be short of money anymore.

You have promised to ask for anything in Your name, then we will accept it. So I now ask for a job to earn $5,000 as soon as possible and I definitely accept it.

Thank you, Jesus.

Amen.

Doing Research

Remember this!

Research is one of the most important things in making money.

Use these questions when you were doing research:
a. Why do you have to start looking for a job?
b. What are skill, knowledge, experience, and ability you want to offer to the company?
c. Do your skill, knowledge, experience, and ability match what the company requested?
d. What is your strategy for finding work?
e. What salary do you ask?
f. When can you get work?

g. Where is the location of the company? Can you work there?
h. Etc.

You must read carefully the various requirements that are requested by the company. Can you fulfill it?

You must find out what the company wants, then give it to them.

You can know what the company wants by looking at the job specification given in the job vacancy. If you can meet all the specifications the company requested, then you can send "a Cover Letter + Resume" to it.

If you cannot meet all the specifications the company requested, then you cannot send "a Cover Letter + Resume" to it. Because it is wasting your time. Unless you can offer better to them.

Example:
JA offers a "link building for SEO" job to increase the ranking of his website.

The author offers the services of making the desired keyword is on page 1 of Google with 100% money back guarantee if it does not work.

Then the author gets a job, which is actually not the expertise of the author (link building). Because he offers better than requested by JA.

Active Income, Passive Income, or Both

Sometimes success takes a long time. Take your time and choose those you can work with for a long time. The key is to pay attention to all the details and keep working your plan until you reach the goals you've set for yourself.

Currently, there are two types of income that is active income and passive income.

Active income is where you get paid for what you do. If you work in an office or do freelance work for clients, then your income is named as an active income.

Passive income is:
1. You do a job once, but you get paid many times. So you get income based on what is generated from the work you are doing now.
2. Work towards something that doesn't just end if you decide to take some time off.
3. Working hard today creates something that will work hard for you tomorrow.

The examples of passive income is you can create a book, program for gameplay, or app. You just make it once. And since the book or game or app is sold then you continue to earn income every month.

Besides making books, software programs, apps, passive income can also be obtained from advertising on blogs, affiliate marketing, renting your home, deposits, buying stock to get an annual dividend, mutual funds, bonds, investing in a startup, etc.

Passive income seems easy and fun, but to get it is not easy. Often you have to spend a lot of time and/or spend a lot of money for investment. Or you do both, then you can get passive income in large numbers.

If you want the passive income from advertising on blogs and affiliate marketing, then you should be able to attract to tens of thousands of people, hundreds of thousands, or millions of people, then you can get a big income. If you are not attracting tens of thousands of people, hundreds of thousands, or millions of people, then you can gets a few dollars to teens dollars. Right?

If you are making books, software programs, or apps, then you should sell for tens of thousands of people, hundreds of thousands, millions of people, or you only can get a few dollars to teens dollars. Right?

If you are renting your home, buying stocks to get an annual dividend, deposits, mutual funds, bonds, investing in a startup, then you must have big capital. If there is no capital, then you cannot get the high passive income. Right?

If people are told to choose between active income and passive income, of course, most people will choose both. Right? Ha…7x

The question now is whether you can get both? Of course, can get both active income and passive income at the same time.

How to Get Both, Active Income and Passive Income

You can get active income and passive income at the same time if you know how to get it.

The trick is as follow:
1. You work to earn active income. A portion of your income is set aside for savings. Once your savings are enough, you can invest in stocks, deposits, or mutual funds to earn passive income.
2. You can take the time to write a book. Once finished, the book can be offered to a large publisher or you publish it yourself to get passive income.
3. You can also pay a ghostwriter to write a book. Once finished, the book can be offered to a large publisher or you publish it yourself to get passive income. You can sell your book in format eBook and paperback to get maximum results.
4. You must say that making a paperback book should spend a lot of money, right? You are wrong. Amazon KDP (Kindle Direct Publishing) gives you the opportunity to publish your book in paperback format for free now. This is the fact wrote on the Amazon website. You can now publish paperback versions of your books with KDP.
5. You can pay a programmer to make a game or an app. Once finished, you can sell it online via Google Play or Apple Store.
6. You can also give your game or app for free. Anyone can use or play it. You advertise in the game or app so you can get passive income
7. Etc.

How to Find a Job Faster

Almost all countries have several websites where you can search for jobs.

Remember this!

Be digital and looking for at the global jobs.

Why? The more websites you browse, the more job vacancies are available. And the more you submit your Cover Letter and Resume, the greater your chances of getting a job.

If the more chance you get a job, the faster you get a job. Right?

So open all the websites that exist below. Find a job that matches your passion. Then, send your Cover Letter and Resume to them.

List of websites that provide job vacancies:

1. Indeed. www.indeed.com.
2. Dribbb. https://dribbble.com/
3. WayUp. https://www.wayup.com/.
4. TARGET Jobs. https://targetjobs.co.uk/
5. Jobs.ie. www.jobs.ie.
6. CAREERBUILDER. www.careerbuilder.com/
7. StartWire. https://www.startwire.com/
8. SimplyHired. http://www.simplyhired.com.
9. Glassdoor. https://www.glassdoor.com/
10. Flexjobs. https://www.flexjobs.com/
11. Jobrapido. Jobrapido.com

12. LinkedIn. https://www.linkedin.com/
13. MediaBistro. https://www.mediabistro.com/
14. JobDiagnosis.com. https://www.jobdiagnosis.com/
15. Craigslist. https://www.craigslist.org/
16. JobsRadar. www.jobsradar.com/
17. Jora. https://www.jora.com/
18. SnagAJob. https://www.snagajob.com.
19. Dice. https://www.dice.com.
20. Career Jet. https://www.careerjet.com/j
21. CareerBliss. https://www.careerbliss.com/
22. Etc.

Of course, there are still tens to hundreds of other websites that have not been mentioned above. You can do research through search engines.

So look for as many websites that provide job vacancies. After that, you can become a member there.

They will send jobs available to you every day. Vacancies are already selected in accordance with your selection/passion.

Remember this!

If you upload your Resume on various websites above, do not ever include your full address, ID card, Credit Card, or your family's name list. Do not let your personnel data misused others.

Create a Great Cover Letter

If you want to get active income, then you have to get one job first. To get a job, then you must apply for work first. And to apply for work, then you must send Cover Letter/**Application Letter** and Resume/**Curriculum Vitae (CV)** first.

Remember this!

You have seconds to make a great first impression.

The first impression is very important. Your Cover Letter and Resume are a reflection of yourself, which is considered to represent your skill, ability, knowledge, experience, quality, and character. So make the boss trust with your knowledge, ability, skill, experience, quality, and character!

Remember this too!

- Be Professional.
- Be Personal.
- Be specific.
- Keep it simple and smart (KISS).
- Use short sentences.
- Use short paragraphs.
- Show your worth.

You must have added value to win the competition through your Cover Letter and Resume. Because if you lose compete, then you will never be called for test and/or interview. And without a test and/or interview, you will never be able to work there.

So prepare your Cover Letter and Resume well. Because you have to win in the first competition, based on the Cover Letter and Resume you sent to the company.

Remember this!

Your Cover Letter and Resume are the first time assessed by the company when they are looking for an employee. So you should be able to attract the attention of a Human Resource Manager. Because if you cannot attract the attention of the Human Resource Manager, then your chances to work there gone with the wind. So you have to win here.

To win in the first competition, then you should be able to make a great Cover Letter and a great Resume first.

How to create a great Cover Letter:

1. Make an interesting design.
2. Make a great first impression.
3. Be Professional.
4. Be Personal.
5. Be nice.
6. Be unique.
7. Put your name in the first sentence.
8. Use first person in your sentences.
9. Use the power words in your sentences. Power words are the words with emotion that makes the audience become happy, sad, angry, sympathy, etc. Of course, the power words you choose are those that can give positive emotions to the boss and/or company.
10. Customize your Cover Letter for different jobs.
11. Show your knowledge, skill, ability, and experience.
12. Show your confidence.
13. Tell them what are the benefits of the company if they recruit you as their employee.
14. Keep it short.

15. Include your resume and photo.
16. Don't repeat your resume.
17. Address to the name at the job description. Or Boss if the job description did not give a name.
18. Send it online.
19. Close your Cover Letter with a call to action. Ask them to try you with a test and/or interview.

Examples of the Great Cover Letters

Here are some examples that you can make a lesson or reference when writing a Cover Letter.

Of course, you do not need to copy and paste this example as you should be able to customize the example below to your needs.

1. Gig: Requires SEO improvement services on the website

Job details:

I Want to develop a service delivery business by increasing SEO on the website to appear on the first page on google search with some keywords as follow: services, delivery, import, wholesale, Guangzhou, China, Jakarta.

Thank you.

Regards.

Cover Letter.

Dear Boss,

With 1 million Rupiah, I will create 1-2 articles that will makes your website a number 1 in Google and/or Yahoo rank with 1 keyword OR 2 POSITIONS ON THE FIRST PAGE OF GOOGLE AND/OR YAHOO. Because I am a specialist to be number 1 on Google and/or Yahoo rankings.

This is the proof:

Keyword: High traffic in one day then is number 1 in Google.

Another proof:

The First Page of Google Ranking With Long-Tail Keywords or My Google+. http://lifeonearthasinheaven.blogspot.co.id/2016/02/the-first-page-of-google-ranking-with.html.

If my articles do not make your website a number 1 on Google and/or Yahoo OR 2 POSITIONS ON THE FIRST PAGE OF GOOGLE AND/OR YAHOO, then I will give you a new article for free to your website becomes number 1 on Google and/or Yahoo OR 2 POSITION ON THE FIRST PAGE OF GOOGLE AND/OR YAHOO.

Thank you.

The Lord Jesus blesses you.

Amen.

After several chats, the author gets the job.

2. Gig: Keyword optimization, link building, strategic content development.

Job details:

- Optimize keywords for website related to art products, for retail and B2B in Indonesia.

- Advice (may include execution) for the creation of content articles (content marketing) related to SEO plans, including the spread of links.

- Preferably domiciled in Semarang to ease the necessary coordination meetings. However, there is no possibility of freelancers from other cities who can work remotely.

- A website, blog, and SEM basic already exist, some basic keywords already in the initial search. Need to add the number of keywords and increase the ranking of existing keywords.

Cover Letter.

Dear Boss,

With 3 million Rupiah, then I will make your website on page 1 Google with 3 keywords.

The proof:

An Article Get 24 number 1 & 53 Page 1 on Google. http://lifeonearthasinheaven.blogspot.co.id/2017/12/an-article-get-24-number-1-51-page-1-on_84.html.

Another proof:

The First Page of Google Ranking With Long-Tail Keywords or My Google+. http://lifeonearthasinheaven.blogspot.co.id/2016/02/the-first-page-of-google-ranking-with.html.

Keyword:

CARGO IMPORT BANGKOK JAKARTA - number 1 in Google.

My books on Amazon:

1. Want More Traffic? 514 Tips to Skyrocket Your Website Traffic and Income Faster.
https://www.amazon.com.au/dp/B0778LTNQ1.

2. How to Start a Business With China.
https://www.amazon.com/dp/B078VHPLXV.

3. How to Create A Great Article for SEO in Three Hours.
https://www.amazon.com.au/dp/B01M0I6WMH.

4. Knowing Jesus Better - the Real Jesus According to Thousands of Verses and Who is Jesus to you?
https://www.amazon.com/dp/B07BJDPR5Y.

Thank you.

Lord Jesus blesses you.

Amen.

After several chats, the author gets the job.

3. Gig: Web SEO

Job details:

Requires specialist SEO.

Criteria:

1. Top 3 Google.

2. Three (3) Keywords.

Please mention the method that will be used and also portfolio/web whoever did.

Cover Letter

Dear Boss,

If you want number 2 on Google and/or Yahoo, then the rate is 2 million Rupiah per keyword.

So 3 keywords: 6 million Rupiah.

The "Token PLN" keyword is numbered 1-2 on Google.

An article from me made Wira Cargo rank #1 on Google through 24 keywords.

The proof:

Do You Want to Be Number 1 on Google? Hire Richard Nata!
http://lifeonearthasinheaven.blogspot.co.id/2017/07/do-you-want-to-be-number-1-on-google.html.

My books on Amazon KDP.

How to Create A Great Article for SEO in Three Hours.

https://www.amazon.com/dp/1521169330?ref_=pe_870760_150889320 – paperback.

https://www.amazon.com/author/richardnata - ebook.

My latest articles:

1. How to Sell at Auction House. http://lauren-gallery.com/2017/06/19/how-to-sell-at-auction-house/

2. How to Buy at Auction House. http://lauren-gallery.com/2017/06/20/how-to-buy-at-auction-house/

3. How to Buy a House at Atlanta Auction House. http://lauren-gallery.com/2017/07/03/how-to-buy-a-house-at-atlanta-auction-house/

4. How to Sell a House at Georgia Auction House. http://lauren-gallery.com/2017/07/07/how-to-sell-a-house-at-georgia-auction-house/

5. How to Buy at Atlanta Fine Antiques. http://lauren-gallery.com/2017/07/07/how-to-buy-at-atlanta-fine-antiques/

6. Oberlo Review: Is Oberlo App Legit? http://lifeonearthasinheaven.blogspot.co.id/2017/05/oberlo-review-is-oberlo-app-legit.html

7. Do You Want to Be Number 1 on Google? Hire Richard Nata! http://lifeonearthasinheaven.blogspot.co.id/2017/07/do-you-want-to-be-number-1-on-google.html

Thank you for your review.

Lord Jesus bless you.

Amen.

After several chats, the author gets the job.

You do not need to copy and paste the 3 examples above.

You'll have to modify it to fit your persona.

You take the point of importance only, that is, if a boss asks A, then give him A+, then you will get a job from him/her.

The three examples above are useful to you if you have had previous work experience.

What if you have never had previous work experience? Often you lose out in competing for the opportunity to work with those who have had work experience. Right? What will you do next?

Example of a great Cover Letter if you have never had previous work experience.

Dear Boss,

I am writing to apply for the position of a Clerk, which I saw advertised on Indeed.com. As a recent graduate of the XXX University, I have a significant background in Accounting. I believe that I am an ideal candidate for this position at your company.

Why me?

This is the reasons:

1. Diligent.
2. Smart.
3. Dedicated.
4. Honest.
5. Thorough.
6. To be responsible.
7. Can be trusted.
8. Hard worker.
9. Ready to work overtime.
10. Always pay attention to details.
11. Can keep the company secrets.

I am excited about the opportunity to join your team as a Clerk.

Try me and you will know that I do not lie to you.

Thank you for your time and consideration.

Sincerely,

Your Signature (hard copy letter)

Your Typed Name

Besides examples of Cover Letters in this book, you should also look at many examples that exist on the internet. After that, make a Cover Letter that bests suits you.

Create a Great Resume

Prepare your resume well. Because you have to make a great Resume or **Curriculum Vitae (CV)**.

Everything listed on the Resume is relevant to the job position.

You should create a great resume so **that makes you stand out from others. So show your worth. And impress your boss.**

How to create a great resume:

1. Be creative and make an interesting design. Make it eye-catching.
2. Customize your Resume for different jobs.
3. Marketing yourself with your resume.
4. Positive attitude.
5. Professional mindset.
6. Be Personnel.
7. Put your name in the first sentence.
8. Use first person in your sentences.
9. Use the power words in your sentences. Power words are the words with emotion that makes the audience become happy, sad, angry, sympathy, etc. Of course, the power words you choose are those that can give positive emotions to the boss and/or company.
10. Put the position you are applying for.
11. Give your color photo.
12. Put your LinkedIn profile.
13. Put your social media profile.
14. Show your knowledge, skill, and experience.
15. Focus with your strong.
16. Tell them what are the benefits of the company if they recruit you as their employee.
17. Keep it easy to read. Make sure the font is not too big or too small (choose a size between 10 and 12).

18. Don't repeat your Cover Letter.
19. Address to Boss.
20. Close your Resume with a call to action. Ask them to try you with a test and/or interview.
21. **Save your resume file as a PDF. Save with your name.**
22. Send it online.

Example of a Great Resume

Everything listed on the Resume is relevant to the position you are applying for.

The contents of your great resume:

1. Name.
2. The position you are applying for.
3. Address.
4. Phone and Skype.
5. Executive Profile.
6. Portfolio.
7. Work Experience.
8. Skill Highlights.
9. LinkedIn.
10. Blogs.
11. Social Media.
12. Interests.
13. Tagline.
14. Responsibilities.
15. Accomplishments.
16. References.
17. Education.

Remember this!

1. An one-page resume is sufficient. Everyone in your job search does not need to see your full-length resume, use the example to write one that's brief and to the point.
2. If a lot of data you want to convey then you can divide it into two or three columns in one page.
3. You must show your strength in your resume. Focus on your skills, ability, expertise, portfolio, work experience, and references. And never show your weakness to the company.
4. You may enter data from your hobbies and interests if it can add value. If not, then you do not need to provide your hobbies and interests in your resume.
5. Create a short, catchy statement that sells you and your skills. Show off your biggest achievements.
6. Add a sentence to bring attention to your value as a candidate. An example is "I am the best person to fill this position."
7. Show the company if you are the right person to fill the position offered. Then you give the reasons.
8. Challenge them with this sentence. Try me a month and you'll be surprised to see what I can do for the company.
9. Don't forget to make your resume unique. Create an interesting design.
10. Never copy-paste your resume for each job you apply for. Because each job offered has a different job description. So you have to adjust your resume to the specifications requested by the company.

Richard Nata

<u>I am the author of 11 books on Amazon</u>: Christianity – Business – Lifestyle – Fiction – Etc

I am a good SEO writer from Indonesia with the first-page of Google specialization.

<u>An article from me made Wira Cargo rank #1 on Google through 24 keywords</u>.

My rate: $300 per article (3,000 words or more)

Email: <u>richardnata0@gmail.com</u> – LinkedIn: <u>https://www.linkedin.com/in/richard-nata-45002686/</u> – Blog: <u>Life on Earth as in Heaven</u>.

Executive Profile
I am an entrepreneur, consultant to Go Public (IPO) in Indonesia Stock Exchange, author, novelist, essayist, blogger, and ghostwriter. My articles, including short stories, published in Magazines and newspapers since 1994. I have written a lot of books, both fiction, and nonfiction. So, I was a professional in writing, both fiction, and non-fiction.

Professional Experience
In 1997, Richard Nata wrote a book entitled "Buku Pintar Mencari Kerja." This book is reprinted as much as 8 times. Through the book, the authors successfully helped tens of thousands of people get jobs at once successful in their careers. They were also successful when moving to work in other places.
Read more: http://richardnata.blogspot.com/2015/01/buku-pintar-mencari-kerja.html
Author – 1995 Until Now
Writer – 1994 Until Now
General Manager, TSP International Co. – Textile Stores – Resign 1994
Finance Manager, PT. Infopen – Export and Import – Resign 1992
Finance Supervisor, PT. Danamon Asuransi – Insurance – Resign 1990
Staff Accountant, PT. Indo Mobil Utama – Car Factory – Resign 1988

Technical Skills
Accounting – Finance – Management – Marketing – Social Media – Translation – Writing – SEO – Business Plan – Slogan – Short Story – Book/eBook – The First Page of Google – Creative Writing – Content Creator – Novel

Education
Atmajaya University with a honor degree in management – Graduated 1993

Tagline
Our expertise and services can solve your problems

Try me and you will be surprised to see the results

You'll have to modify it to fit your persona.

The example above are useful to you if you have had previous work experience.

What if you have never had previous work experience?

You can use the Resume above. But you should omit the data about the Professional Experience. Because you have no previous work experience.

Maybe you can write your experience in organizing or your experience whiles working internship.

Make Your Cover Letter and Resume Become One Page

Remember this!

1. The higher the position in the company, the busier they are.
2. The bigger the company the busier the management.
3. Sharpen your Cover Letter and Resume.
4. Be Professional.
5. Be Personnel.
6. Be nice.
7. It would be nice if your Cover Letter and Resume are merged into one page so it does not take much time from the boss. Right?
8. One page of your data coupled with a good design will make your chances to get a job bigger. Right?
9. Your challenge to the boss will make you welcome to work there. Ha...7x

Source image: https://www.pexels.com/photo/graphs-job-laptop-papers-590016/

Use the Power of Words

Remember this!

You should always use the power of words to improve the emotions of your boss.

The more power of words you give, the better.

Always use the power of words on:

a. Your great Cover Letter.

b. Your great Resume.

c. Your video profile.

d. Your profile on LinkedIn.

e. Your profile on other social media.

Examples of the power of word:

1. 101 Ways to Make Your First $5,000 – a good title.

101 Amazing Ways to Make Your First $5,000 Faster – a great title.

Amazing and faster are the power of words.

2. 50 Amazing Ways to Conquer Your Fear.

Amazing and conquer are the power of words.

3. The Best Way to Stop Watching Porn Today.

The best way and today are the power of words.

4. Mission: Impossible (a series of action spy films), Die Hard (movie), Spice Girls (English pop girl group), and Girl Power (Spice Girls popularized the slogan in the mid-1990s) are examples of the other power of words.

So you can start sprinkling your power words now. Because it will increase your chances of winning the competition to get a job.

Always Check and Recheck

Things that can goes wrong will goes wrong. Never assume, but always check and verify. So always check and recheck twice or more.

You should edit and proofread twice or more before send your Cover Letter and Resume.

Why? Because after reading over and over again, then you can see typos, spelling, or grammar. Or you can see the error based on sentence structure. You can fix it immediately.

15 Simple Ways to Attract the Company's Attention

You should be tested and interviewed first. And to get tested and interview opportunities, then you should be able to attract the attention of the boss first.

How to communicate what makes you special so the boss's say yes.

15 simple ways to attract the company's attention is:

1. Create your video profile then upload to YouTube. After that, give the link in your Cover Letter or Resume.
2. Give your great Cover Letter.
3. Give your great Resume.
4. Give your great LinkedIn profile.
5. Show your strength, skill, ability, knowledge, and experience.
6. Be Professional.
7. Be Personnel.
8. Be nice.
9. Positive attitude.
10. Professional mindset.
11. Do not show your weaknesses.

12. Give your plan to the company.
13. Give your plan to the future.
14. Give many reasons why the company should choose you over the others.
15. Give the company a challenge to hire you.

Create Your Video Profile Then Upload to YouTube

If you want to win the competition by getting a job, then you should make a video that tells a story about yourself. Because almost everyone like a story telling.

In the video, you can:

1. Deliver value.
2. Tell your story.
3. Build trust.
4. Solve a problem.
5. Get results.
6. Make the boss trust with your knowledge, ability, experience, and skill.
7. Tell them who are you and why you are worth it for them. If you successfully do this then you will be invited to join their company.

In the video, sharing your personnel stories and other details about your skill, ability, expertise, experience, and what you do in your life, so your boss instantly gets who you are, what you stand for, how you want to contribute to the world and how you can help them (the company). Then you can create a powerful, emotional connection with your boss.

Boss wants to hear you speak about what you already know.

Examples:

1. What was an "a-ha" moment for you when you started your job in their company?
2. Show respect to the company.
3. How do you want to help/contribute through your knowledge, skill, ability, and experience? Show your worth.
4. What motivated you to join with them? Showing your boss what you mean and not just telling them, gives your stories depth and emotional power.
5. Do not forget to use the power of words whenever you can. So, your words can evoke emotions from the boss or maybe even change his mind and/or life.
6. Show the strength of your character in the video. People will forget what you said. But people just remember what you did!
7. Character is what somebody still trust you, when you do wrong. Your character in the video plays an important role for your future. "Mental toughness can take you to the top, and mental weakness straight to the bottom!" – John Schiefer.
8. If you are applying for a job as a Manager or a Director then you can say this. Let's we create a better future for the company together. I want to be there as part of your team.

9. If you wanna stay as a winner-Leader so you must have what they have. Do you know what winner have? "Character!" So improve your character now.
10. Don't hesitate to share your future vision story with the boss in your video.
11. Be Professional.
12. Be Personnel.
13. Be nice.
14. Don't forget to ask the boss to try you. And give him/her a challenge that he/she cannot refuse.

Remember this!

You have seconds to make a great first impression.

You can say that you will appreciate everyone who interacts with you and the company because they are important people.

Matthew {7:12} Therefore all things whatsoever ye would that men should do to you, do ye even so to them: for this is the law and the prophets.

So if you want to be appreciated then you have to respect others first.

Remember this!

A boss uses his/her employees because he/she is looking for a solution to his/her company problems. If your video is in-depth enough to answer all the company problems, then he/she will hire you asap (as soon as possible).

Sharing stories in your life helps you communicate in a way that is persuasive, compelling, and memorable. You'll grab the spotlight and get heard by your boss.

After that, you can upload to YouTube. Then you include your video profile link in your email or Cover Letter or Resume.

If you do it, then you will shine among other candidates because you are more innovative than the other candidates.

What you should record in the video:

1. Show with confidence.

2. A glimpse of your life.

3. Your name.

4. Your education.

5. Your work experience.

6. Your knowledge.

7. Your skills and ability.

8. Hobby.

9. Be Yourself.

10. Be enthusiastic.

11. Tell a story. We all LOVE stories, right? So your story can help you find many companies to test and/or interview you. So what's gonna happen next? A job you want it. Ha...7x

Besides the 11 things above, the contents of the video that will makes your boss memorable are to provide answers for questions that will be asked boss during the interview.

List of frequently asked questions by the boss at the interview:

1. Briefly describe yourself.
2. What strengths do you have?
3. Why should the company hires you?
4. What are you going to do with an annoying co-worker?
5. Tell what you can do for the company.
6. How do you see your career 5 years into the future?

If you do this, then the boss will give you a plus. Because you have given the answer before the boss asked. And he/she will like you because you think more advanced than the other candidates. And your video helps your boss get to know the real you. **This creates an extraordinary emotional connection.**

So create your life story that powerful emotional investment today.

Remember this!

If there are tens or hundreds of thousands or millions who watch and love your video then you can get passive income through YouTube advertising.

So start creating a video about yourself and upload it on YouTube today. Ha...7x

Use Your LinkedIn Profile to Attract Boss and/or Headhunter

LinkedIn is a social media for businesses and professionals.

LinkedIn has more than 500 million members in 200 countries now. And more than 106 million members are active. It covers 150 industries and over 400 economic areas classified by the service.

The members of LinkedIn used for professional networking, including employers posting jobs and job seekers posting their CVs.

LinkedIn allows its members to create business connections, search for jobs, and find the potential clients.

Based on the various data above, then you should create an account at LinkedIn. Then you create a profile as well as possible. The more professional your profile is, the better.

The author's profile on LinkedIn is mediocre, but the author gets 3 job offers, one of which has transferred money before contacting the author.

Besides the authors, many executives have moved to another company after getting a job offer with much better facilities elsewhere. And the Headhunters get the executives data from their profiles on LinkedIn and other sources.

So never forget to brand yourself on LinkedIn. And start branding yourself now.

You never know, what offer you will get if you successfully branding yourself.

How to Build Your Personal Brand on LinkedIn

You should start building yourself on LinkedIn to make you look more professional.

Branding yourself is sharing about who you are, what you loved, skills, ability, knowledge, experience, character, and passion with people who want to hear about it.

You can also share your articles, images, memes, infographics, and videos to showcase your abilities, knowledge, experience, character, and skills.

Remember this!

- Always using your data to brand yourself.
- You can use interesting design to strengthen when branding yourself.
- Branding yourself can impress your boss.
- Building your personnel brand on LinkedIn takes some work, but it could create your next job opportunity.
- Use keywords and hashtags so that your data are easy to find.

How to build your personal brand on LinkedIn:

1. Always update your LinkedIn accounts.
2. Positive attitude.
3. Professional mindset.
4. Job experience. Write about your working experience. Starting from your last job. Do not forget to include starting work from month and year, the company name, work location, your position, and a brief description of your job description.
5. Use SEO (Search Engine Optimization) and hashtags on your profile.
6. Identify your area of expertise and find the right groups.
7. Meet new people in LinkedIn and build professional relationships with them.
8. Make a friend with the influencers. You can become their followers.
9. Engage regularly with them.
10. You can like, comments, and share their contents and/or status.
11. You can also create your own content to share with your group. Create and share-worthy content. Add amazing images and/or videos.
12. If necessary, then create and curate engaging content. So you can share your content on a regular basis.
13. Building your network on LinkedIn. Import your contacts (friends, family, neighbors, and customers/clients).
14. You can open a thread to start a discussion. Ask questions to members of the group.
15. Keep it positive. Do some good.
16. Be confident.
17. Expand your skills, ability, experience, and knowledge.
18. Be active in the group you are following.

19. You can search for jobs through job openings on LinkedIn. Find new opportunities and careers.
20. Etc.

We recommend that you create a Resume on your profile, but your Resume in LinkedIn is more detailed than one Resume page while looking for a job.

Why? Because you will give a link from your Resume to your LinkedIn account.

If necessary, you create one or more videos that show your skills. Then you can upload to your LinkedIn.

Remember this!

Never manipulate your data in your LinkedIn account because when you are agreed to work in a company then you have to give all your data to them. So do not let the data you provide is different with your data in LinkedIn. Because you can be fired for faking your data.

Now you know how to win the LinkedIn branding game. So what are you waiting for? Fix your LinkedIn profile now.

Remember this!

Keep your branding consistent across platforms, like Facebook, Twitter, Instagram, etc. But the impact you get is not as good as if you are branding on LinkedIn.

Never be racist, whenever and wherever. Include in your status in social media. Because the company will sees your accounts in social media. If they find you racist, then you can be banned from working in their company forever.

23 Golden Rules of Seeking a Job

The author believes if you do the golden rule below, then you will get a job quickly.

23 golden rules when looking for a job:

1. Pray to God.
2. Doing a Research.
3. Talk less, do more.
4. Create your video profile. Then upload to YouTube. Then you include your video profile link in your email or Cover Letter or Resume.
5. Create your LinkedIn profile. Then you include your LinkedIn profile link in your Resume.
6. Start making a great Cover Letter and Resume.
7. Start an email with the recipient's name or title. If you do not know, then replace it with the word "Boss." Because everyone likes to be called as boss.
8. Introduce yourself in one or two short sentences. You can write based on your perspective.
9. Give your photo in accordance with the company's dress code policy.
10. Don't forget to check and recheck your Cover Letter and Resume! Check for errors in data, typo, spelling, grammar, or sentence structure.
11. Never copy paste your Cover Letter and Resume. You should customize your Cover Letter and Resume with the given job descriptions.

12. Send your Cover Letter and Resume every day. If necessary, send hundreds to thousands of your Cover Letter and Resume every day until you get a job.
13. Email should use your full name. Use richardnata0@gmail.com instead of rich123@gmail.com.
14. Your email should use Yahoo or Gmail.
15. Never stop applying for work until you get a job. Because the rejection is part of looking for a job. Almost every single employee has had a rejected when they're looking for a job.
16. Never stop applying for work until you get a job. Although you have been tested and interviewed at a company. Because you could have failed to work there for one reason or another.
17. Schedule your time to apply for a job every day.
18. You need to set clear daily goals. An example is daily you send your Cover Letters and Resume to 250 companies. Then stick to it.
19. Use the flexibility. An example is you start opening job advertisements and apply for work from 9 am to 5 pm. But you can be flexible, apply for work at 7 am or 8 pm.
20. If you cannot get a full-time job in a company for one reason or another, then you can start looking for a part-time job as a full-time freelancer.
21. If you cannot get a full-time job or part-time job, then you should create a job for yourself.
22. Ask for help from your parents, friends, family, or neighbors, so they would recommend you to the company, so you can get a job faster.
23. Remove all your racist words in social media. Why? Because companies sometimes do personnel

background checks against their prospective employees.

Do a Job That No One Else Wants

If you really want to get your first $5,000 faster, then it helps you consider the work that other people do not want.

You will quickly get work and earn money every month because most people avoid the job. Therefore, you have no rivals or just a few rival when applying for the job.

The job that no one else wants:

1. Bathing a dead body.
2. Make up a dead body.
3. Hearse Driver.
4. Undertaker.
5. Garbageman.
6. Street Sweeper.
7. Dish Washer.
8. Selling at a Flea Market.
9. Etc.

Do Not Take the Job That Enslaving You

Remember this!

You are not a slave, therefore, do not take the job that enslaves you unless you have to do it.

The list of jobs that enslave you because the wages are so small:
1. Click and/or read ads.
2. Watch TV or video.
3. Filling survey.
4. Microworker.
5. Download smartphone apps.
6. Data entry jobs.
7. Copy paste jobs.
8. Join a virtual jury.
9. Etc.

If you want to earn more money, the company offers you to buy referrals. But you will never get a huge income evens if you have bought referrals. Therefore, do not ever want to be enslaved by the company in this way. Ha...7x

Similarly, the work that pays you with the voucher and/or gift card.

Instead of you pick up a job that enslaves you, you better work as an internship.

Internship Jobs

An internship can be a valuable first step towards a great career.

Many companies that offer internships to Students and/or people. They do so to save costs because companies do not have to pay for the work internship or pay below the minimum wage.

If you are a Student and want to work, the authors suggest that taking internships at companies that want to pay for the internship. Because you work for a company, so the companies should pay you.

Here's a list of websites that show the work of the internship:
a. Indeed. www.indeed.com/q-Internship-jobs.html.
b. WayUp. https://www.wayup.com/.
c. TARGET Jobs. https://targetjobs.co.uk/internships.
d. TalentEgg. https://talentegg.ca/. Jobs for Canadian students and new graduates.
e. Bloomberg. https://www.bloomberg.com/careers.
f. InternJobs. http://www.internjobs.com.
g. Jobs.ie. www.jobs.ie/work_experience_internship_jobs.aspx. Jobs in Ireland.
h. The Guardian (media in the UK). https://jobs.theguardian.com/
i. CAREERBUILDER. www.careerbuilder.com/jobs/keyword/internship.
j. SimplyHired. http://www.simplyhired.com.
k. Boston. http://www.bostonmagazine.com/internships.
l. BAREFOOT STUDENT. http://www.barefootstudent.com.

Look for internships jobs in your city. Then send your Cover Letter and Resume to them. If they refuse, then send it to other companies. Try to try again, until you get a job.

401 Professional Jobs That You Can Apply For

The list of jobs that you can apply for:

1. Accountant.
2. Actor/Actress.

3. Actuary.
4. Administrator.
5. Administrator of a Website.
6. Advertising Manager.
7. Advisor.
8. Agent.
9. Agronomist.
10. Aide.
11. Air Steward.
12. Air Traffic Controller.
13. Aircraft Mechanic.
14. Ambassador.
15. Animator.
16. Anthropologist.
17. Archeologist.
18. Architect.
19. Art Critic.
20. Art Director.
21. Art Gallery Curator.
22. Art Maker.
23. Art Photographer.
24. Artist.
25. Assessor.
26. Assistant.
27. Assistant Accounting Manager.
28. Assistant Front Office Manager.
29. Assistant Housekeeper.
30. Assistant Marketing Manager.
31. Assistant Professor.
32. Astronaut.
33. Astronomer.
34. Athlete.
35. Attendant.
36. Attorney.

37. Auctioneer.
38. Auditor.
39. Author.
40. Babysitter.
41. Background Singer.
42. Baker.
43. Banker.
44. Barber.
45. Bassist.
46. Beautician.
47. Beekeeper.
48. Bellboy.
49. Bellhop.
50. Bellmen.
51. Bibliographer.
52. Biologist.
53. Blacksmith.
54. Blogger.
55. Bodyguard.
56. Botanist.
57. Bricklayer.
58. Broker.
59. Builder.
60. Building Inspector.
61. Bus Driver.
62. Businessman.
63. Butcher.
64. Butler.
65. Buzzer.
66. Caddie.
67. Calligrapher.
68. Cameraman.
69. Caretaker.
70. Car Mechanic.

71. Carpenter.
72. Carver.
73. Cashier.
74. Cat Caretaker.
75. Celebrity.
76. Chambermaids.
77. Chauffeur.
78. Cheerleader.
79. Chef.
80. Chief Concierge.
81. Chief Information Officer.
82. Chief Reservation Officer.
83. Chief Uniformed Service.
84. Choreographer.
85. Circus Artist.
86. Civil Servant.
87. Cleaner.
88. Clerk.
89. Coach.
90. Cobbler.
91. College Teacher.
92. Comedian.
93. Comic Artist.
94. Company Director.
95. Composer.
96. Computer Engineer.
97. Computer Operator.
98. Computer Repair Technician.
99. Conductor (Orchestral).
100. Conductor (Tram/Bus).
101. Confectioner.
102. Construction Worker.
103. Consultant.
104. Cook.

105. Cook Medical.
106. Copywriter.
107. Correspondent.
108. Craftsman.
109. Dancer.
110. Dean.
111. Decorator.
112. Dental Nurse.
113. Dental Surgeon.
114. Dentist.
115. Designer.
116. Detective.
117. Dietician.
118. Digger.
119. Diplomat.
120. Director.
121. Diver.
122. Docker.
123. Doctor.
124. Dog Trainer.
125. Doorkeeper.
126. Doorman.
127. Dockworker.
128. Dramatist.
129. Dressmaker.
130. Dress Designer.
131. Driver.
132. Driver Bus.
133. Driving Instructor.
134. Dropshipper.
135. Drummer.
136. Ecologist.
137. Economist.
138. Editor.

139. Educator.
140. Electrician.
141. Employee.
142. Engineer.
143. English Teacher.
144. Entrepreneur.
145. Entertainer.
146. Ergonomist.
147. Ethnographer.
148. Event Organizer (EO).
149. Farm Worker.
150. Farmer.
151. Fashion Designer.
152. Film Critic.
153. Film Director.
154. Film Editor.
155. Film Set Designer.
156. Financial Analyst.
157. Financial Officer.
158. Fine Artist.
159. Fire Officer.
160. Firefighter.
161. Fish Farmer.
162. Fisherman.
163. Fishmonger.
164. Flight Attendant.
165. Flight Engineer.
166. Forester.
167. Freelancer.
168. Front Office Cashier.
169. Front Office Manager.
170. Furniture Designer.
171. Gardener.
172. Geneticist.

173. Geographer.
174. Goldsmith.
175. Graphic designer.
176. Guest Relations Officer.
177. Guitarist.
178. Gym Instructor.
179. Hairdresser.
180. Handyman.
181. Hatter.
182. Headmaster.
183. Herbalist.
184. Historian.
185. History Teacher.
186. Housewife.
187. Host.
188. Hotel Porter.
189. Hydrologist.
190. Illustrator.
191. Inspector.
192. Interior Designer.
193. Interpreter.
194. Investigator.
195. Janitor.
196. Jeweler.
197. Jewelry Designer.
198. Journalist.
199. Judge.
200. Keyboard Player (Keyboardist).
201. Knitter.
202. Labor.
203. Land Surveyor.
204. Landlord/Landlady.
205. Laptop Repair Technician.
206. Lawyer.

207. Lecturer.
208. Legal Adviser.
209. Librarian.
210. Lifeguard.
211. Longshoreman.
212. Machinery Inspector.
213. Maid.
214. Make-up Artist.
215. Management Accountant.
216. Management Consultant.
217. Manager.
218. Manicurist.
219. Marine.
220. Marine Engineer.
221. Marionette (Manipulator).
222. Marketing Manager.
223. Mason.
224. Masseur.
225. Master of Ceremonies (MC).
226. Mathematician.
227. Math Teacher.
228. Mechanic.
229. Mechanical Engineer.
230. Mechatronic Engineer.
231. Merchant.
232. Metallurgist.
233. Meteorologist.
234. Metrologist.
235. Microbiologist.
236. Midwife.
237. Miller.
238. Miner.
239. Model.
240. Modiste.

241. Museum Curator.
242. Music Director.
243. Music Teacher.
244. Musician.
245. Nanny.
246. Naval Designer.
247. News Anchor.
248. News Presenter.
249. Newspaper Editor.
250. Night Manager.
251. Notary Public.
252. Novelist.
253. Nurse.
254. Nursery Nurse.
255. Nutritionist.
256. Office Boy/Office Girl.
257. Operator.
258. Optician.
259. Ore Crusher.
260. Paediatrician.
261. Page Girl.
262. Painter.
263. Park Ranger.
264. Pastor.
265. Patent Agent.
266. Peddler.
267. Pedicurist.
268. Performer.
269. Personal Assistant.
270. Pet Sitter.
271. Pharmacist.
272. Philosopher.
273. Photographer.
274. Physicist.

275. Physiotherapist.
276. Pianist.
277. Piano tuner.
278. Pilot.
279. Playwright.
280. Plumber.
281. Poet.
282. Policeman.
283. Police Assistant.
284. Police Investigator.
285. Politician.
286. Porter.
287. Postman.
288. Priest.
289. Principal.
290. Prison Officer.
291. Private Teacher.
292. Producer.
293. Professor.
294. Project Manager for Events.
295. Provost.
296. Proofreader.
297. Programmer.
298. Prosecutor.
299. Psychiatrist.
300. Psychologist.
301. Public Notary.
302. Public Speaker.
303. Puppeteer.
304. Purchasing Officer.
305. Quality Control Technician.
306. Quality Inspector.
307. Quilter.
308. Radiologist.

309. Ranger.
310. Real Estate Agent.
311. Receptionist.
312. Rector.
313. Referee.
314. Repairer.
315. Reporter.
316. Researcher.
317. Safety Engineer.
318. Sailor.
319. Sales Assistant.
320. Sales Manager.
321. Sales Representative.
322. Salesman.
323. Scenarist.
324. Scientist.
325. Script Editor.
326. Sculptor.
327. Sea Captain.
328. Secretary.
329. Security.
330. Security Guard.
331. Seller.
332. Selling at a flea market.
333. Sell the Secondhand Stuff.
334. SEO Writer.
335. Sewer.
336. Shepherd.
337. Sheriff.
338. Shipmaster.
339. Shoemaker.
340. Shop Assistant.
341. Showman.
342. Singer.

343. Smartphone Repair Technician.
344. Social Media Manager.
345. Social Worker.
346. Sociologist.
347. Soldier.
348. Solicitor.
349. Songwriter.
350. Staff Accounting.
351. Staff Finance.
352. Staff Marketing.
353. Staff Writer.
354. Statistician.
355. Stevedore.
356. Steward/Stewardess.
357. Stockbroker.
358. Storekeeper.
359. Stuntman/Stuntwoman.
360. Superintendent.
361. Surgeon.
362. Tailor.
363. Tablet Repair Technician.
364. Tax Consultant.
365. Taxi Driver.
366. Teacher.
367. Technician.
368. Telephone Operator.
369. Telephonist.
370. Teller.
371. Tour Guide.
372. Trader.
373. Traffic Officer.
374. Train Driver.
375. Train Operator.
376. Trainer.

377. Translator.
378. Travel Agent.
379. TV Cameraman.
380. TV Presenter.
381. Umpire.
382. University Teacher.
383. Valet.
384. Vet.
385. Veterinarian.
386. Veterinarian Technicians.
387. Video Editor.
388. Video Maker.
389. Violinist.
390. Waiter/Waitress.
391. Watchmaker.
392. Weaver.
393. Web Designer.
394. Website Administrator.
395. Welder.
396. Wigmaker.
397. Wikipedia Page Creation.
398. Wrangler.
399. Writer.
400. YouTuber.
401. Zookeeper.
402. Etc.

Besides the 401 professional jobs above, of course, there are other jobs that have not been included in the list.

Actually, there are still dozens of professions that have not been included in the list above.

Test

If you win the competition through your Cover Letter and Resume, then you will be called by the company to follow a series of tests.

You will be tested for skills, abilities, and knowledge in the field you are applying for. In addition, the company will also test your IQ (Intelegent Quotient).

Basically, the test consists of:

1. Written test. It is usually a question about the job problems appropriate to the position you will be applying for. Show them, how your skills, ability, knowledge, and experience relate specifically to this job. Show them, why you are the best candidate compared to other candidates.

2. Skills and knowledge test. Usually a case question. Can you solve a case faced by the company? You should answer by combining theory, facts, and assumptions.

3. IQ test. A test to measure your intelligence and intellectual abilities.

You should prepare yourself as best as possible because the higher your score, then the greater your chances to work there.

Each company has different test methods. You should be prepared for any type of test. Because your work and salary are determined by your test results.

4. The medical test.

Not many companies require you to be tested before you are accepted to work there.

So always prepare yourself to learn when you will face a test. And be confident and believe in yourself.

Interview

You should get enough sleep before doing the test and/or interview because if you look pale and sleepy due to lack of sleep, then the judgment on your personality will be bad.

Here is a list of frequently asked questions at the interview:

1. Can you tell me about yourself?

2. Why should we hire you? Why do you think you would be a good fit for the job?

3. What strengths do you have?

4. What are your weaknesses? And how do you overcome it?

5. Have you ever been in conflict in your previous jobs? And how do you handle it?

6. Can you work together as a team?

7. What are you going to do with an annoying co-worker?

8. How do you see your career 5 years into the future?

9. Why did you resign from your old job?

10. How much salary do you want?

11. Are you planning to get married and have children soon?

12. Are you happy with your wife/husband?

13. How much time do you dedicated to educating yourself and your own skills so can you succeed?

14. Your plan, how long have you worked for our company?

15. What is your commitment to the company?

16. Any questions you want to ask? Your boss wants to hear you speak about what you already know the company.

17. Etc.

While being interviewed, you should be able to answer quickly all the questions provided. Therefore, prepare yourself if you are called for an interview.

Remember this!

- Do not ever say that you cannot stand working in the previous company. But let's say that you are looking for a new challenge in the company you are currently applying for.
- Do not ever say if you want to do anything to be agreed to work there. Because it will destroy your image and self-esteem.

How to Make Your Interviewer Impressed While Interviewing You

At the time of interview, sometimes you are interviewed by one or a few Interviewer.

Sometimes you are interviewed by:

1. A Human Resources Manager or Branch Manager or Head Factory Manager.
2. Your Manager candidate.
3. The Director.
4. Your Boss candidate (the owner of the company).
5. All them.

How to make your interviewer impressed while interviewing you:

1. You should make preparations before the time you are interviewed.
2. Remove all negative posts from your social media. Examples, you often create or spread the news hoax. Or you often post the racist words. Or you often spread hatred toward other groups.
3. You should do the exercises with your family or friends. Train answering questions that may be asked of you.
4. Research as much as you can about the company you are applying for.
5. Comes one half before the specified time.

6. Dress neatly according to the position you are applying for. If you're interviewing for a professional, managerial, or executive position you should always wear a suit.
7. If you are a woman then do not makeup excessively.
8. Do not forget to make the work-appropriate shoes.
9. Be friendly to everyone you meet.
10. Handshake all them.
11. Show respects to all them.
12. Always smiling at the other person.
13. You sit with the upright position with both shoulders aligned. It shows your confidence.
14. Keep your body language. Suppose you never yawn when interviewed. Do not make the sound of your fingers.
15. Notice the body language of the interviewers. Look at their eyes and stay focus on all the time. Your eyes do not look to the right and to the left, but focus on the eyes of your interviewers.
16. Answer all questions quickly. Answer with short and clear words, so you look a professional.
17. Do not look nervous when answering their questions.
18. If you have worked elsewhere, then do not vilify where you work. Why? Because the interviewer will knows if you are not working there, then you will vilify their company to another party. Of course, they do not want you to vilify their company to another party in the future.
19. If they ask you to ask, then you can ask in a polite and elegant way.
20. You can ask about their working hours, overtime, bonus, etc.
21. Ask them when you are given certainty whether you are asked to join the company or not. Ask them to tell you even if they refuse you.

22. After the interview ends, then do not forget to shake hands and thank them all.
23. Follow up with email or phone after a few days.

Lessons Learned: What a Lost Test and/or Interview Really Tells You

If you fail in a test, then you should study harder when facing the next test at another company. If not, you can fail again in the face of the next test with another company.

If you fail in an interview, then you should practice harder when facing the next interview at another company. If not, you can fail again in the face of the next interview with another company.

Evaluate yourself. What causes you to fail during the test/interview. Then fix it.

You are on the right track if you experience rejection when you are applying for a job.

Rejection doesn't mean you're bad or wrong – it means that you're learning and it's part of the process. In the beginning, you're probably not going to be great, but as time goes by, your skills will increase, and you will start to see results.

And if your next test/interview still fails, then evaluate and fix it again.

Always repeat the above method, until you are agreed to work in a company.

Remember this!

It's time to move on and see if you can get a better accepted elsewhere. Because a rejection is part of the process and that is the part you have to go through before you can become a successful worker.

Salary Strategy

Salary/wage is a sensitive issue for people. Therefore, never tell how much your salary to your office friends. Because if your salary is greater than them, then they will be envious of you. Whereas if your salary is smaller than them, then you will be underestimated by them.

Similarly, salary will you ask when you are looking for work. The salary issues are a very sensitive issue.

If you ask too high, then you cannot compete with those who dare to be paid less. Conversely, if you ask too low, then you will be difficult to manage money for your routine needs every month.

Therefore, you must have a strategy when discussing your salary.

Here's your strategy when discussing your salary:

1. If you have never worked, then you should not question how much your salary every month. So take it. You should seek the work experience first.

2. If you've worked before, but now you are unemployed, then you should not question how much your salary every month. You should work again first because you are much better off than no job.
3. If you've worked before and currently you're still working, then you should ask for a salary that is much larger than the salary in the last place you work. You can ask for 1.5 - 2.5 times your last salary.
4. If you are offered a job by a boss or a headhunter, then you should ask 3 - 10 times your last salary.

Why Didn't You Get a Job There?

17 reasons you didn't get the job after testing and interview:

1. Come Too Late.

2. Wrong costume or not dressed neatly.

3. Do not know what position you are applying there.

4. Do not carry a pen when you come there to follow a test.

5. Not confident.

6. Excessive anxiety.

7. You are considered stupid for not being able to answer the questions given.

8. Caught lying.

9. Badmouthing the previous company.

10. Looks less convincing because you cannot or slowly answer one or more questions.

11. Not polite.

12. Arrogant.

13. Lack of insight about the company.

14. The salary you are asking is too high.

15. There are other candidates who are better than you.

16. You failed the medical test.

17. You are considered unsuitable to work there.

Tips for Success Facing Your First Day Working

The first day of your work is very important because your success working there is determined by your first day.

Why? Your boss, manager, and co-workers will judge your character and the assessment begin on the first day you work there.

Tips for success facing your first day working:

1. Do not be late to the office on your first day of work.

2. Introduce yourself to everyone in the office. Handshake all them.

3. Be friendly to everyone in the office. Show respects to all them.

4. Many ask your senior or manager.

5. Ask politely.

6. Eat together during the meal times. Especially with employees in the same division as you.

7. Do not lie.

8. Do not gossip.

9. Can work together as a team.

10. Quickly adjust to your work environment.

11. Be patient if you get bullied from your senior.

12. Follow your manager's lead.

13. Be enthusiastic with your job.

14. Always smiling at the other person. Always smiling when chased by seniors.

15. Don't like to mumble, swear, or get angry.

19 Golden Rules when Working

After accepted work, then you should work well so that you are not fired.

Not only that, you should try to be able to ride the position quickly so that your salary can goes up quickly too. Right? He...7x

19 golden rule when working:

1. Learn how to be a friend with your colleagues and your manager.
2. Can adapt to the work environment and office friends.
3. Have passion in work.
4. Diligent work.
5. Talk less, do more.
6. Good ethics.
7. Communicative.
8. Open minded.
9. Discipline.
10. Hard working. Ready to work hard.
11. Ready to work overtime if necessary.
12. Honest.
13. Be Responsible.
14. Reliable. Can be trusted.
15. Having the good attitude towards people.
16. Always improve knowledge, ability, and skills.
17. Can work as a team.
18. Willing to be assigned out of town or abroad.

19. Stop making excuses when making mistakes in working at the office. You better confess wrong and apologize. After that, promise not to make the same mistakes again in the future.

"Education is the most powerful weapon which you can use to change the world." — Nelson Mandela.

When It's Time to Move Jobs

There are many reasons for someone to move to another job at another company.

Remember this!

You do not rush to move to another company and/or you do not like to move the job to another company. Why? Job doesn't always come easy. And your track record will be bad if you often move the job to another company.

According to the author, you should work for 3-5 years, then you move to another company. Why? Because you will become an expert in the field if you want to work for 3-5 years before you move to another company. After that, you can ask for the better salary at another company whiles you are applying for a job there.

So be patient and look for the best deals in salary.

Never Resign Until You Get a High Salary from the New Job or You Are Fired

Remember this!

If you already feel uncomfortable working in a company then hang on first. Do not rush to send a letter of resignation.

Finding work is not easy. Moreover, get a job with a high salary. Therefore, never resign until you get a high salary from the new job or you are fired.

You should still work there while sending multiple Cover Letters + Resume to many other companies.

After you get a job in another company, then you submit a resignation letter to the company where you are working now.

Why?

- This way will keep you work and earn a monthly salary.
- Conversely, if you stop working first, then you should become an unemployed before you are agreed to work for another company. Right?
- This way does not pose a problem if you are directly agreed to work elsewhere. Conversely, if it takes a few months or several years, then you can work elsewhere, then you will have the difficulty money because you

do not get a monthly salary again after stopping work. Right?

If You Are Fired, Then Drop Your Ego and Start to Move on Yourself

What if you get fired for one thing or another? Never pity yourself. Never give up too.

It's time to move on and see if you can get a better accepted elsewhere.

Maybe your ego will says this:

1. If my friend knows I was fired. I'm so ashamed.
2. They'll think I'm stupid.
3. I don't want my family and friends to know I am scared about my future.

Ignore and drop down your ego and start to move on yourself.

Everyone knows that getting fired is very painful. But do not grieve for too long because time keeps going.

Remember this!

Even if you get fired, you do not start from zero again. You already have work experience in the company.

Encourage you because you can start looking for work again at another company.

You've done it and you've managed to get a job in a company. So you can do it again.

In order for your time is not only used to find a full time job then it helps you start working as a full-time freelancer.

If you want to become a full-time freelancer, then the author has prepared this book.

How to Make Your First $5,000 Faster as a Full-Time Freelancer.

You can read, study, and practice the contents of the book above, in order for you to succeed as a full-time freelancer.

Ready, Set, Go!

In every race, these words are often shouted "ready, set, go!"

There are also those who use this word "on your mark, get set, go!"

You have read and studied the contents of this book. So you can start practicing now.

Start searching and applying for work today so you can get Your First $ 5,000 Faster. Right?

So you can "ready, set, and go" to get your first $5,000. Ha...7x

Conclusion

Looking for a job is easy.

All you do is:

1. Setup your revenue target.

2. Choose a job you love.

3. Pray to God.

4. Doing a research and find, the companies that looking for the employees.

5. Start writing your Cover Letter and Resume.

6. Making your video profile.

7. Upload your video profile on YouTube.

8. Build your personnel brand on LinkedIn.

9. Customize your Cover Letter and Resume with the given job descriptions.

10. Schedule your time to apply for much more jobs every day.

11. If you fail, then do not give up. Learn more and develop your skills, ability, experience, and knowledge. Try to try again, until you get a job.

12. Never stop applying for work until you get a job.

Making your first $5,000 is easy.

All you do is:

1. The faster you start looking for a job, then the faster you get a job.

2. Working until you make your first $5,000.

3. Never resign until you get a high salary from a new job or you are fired.

So making your first $5,000 is easy, since you are willing to work hard and use the best of your ability, skill, experience, and knowledge.

And do not forget to give thanks to God every day.

Prayer and work (ora et labora). Do not worry. Believe God with all your heart.

Have not I commanded thee? Be strong and of a good courage; be not afraid, neither be thou dismayed: for the LORD thy God [is] with thee whithersoever thou goest (Joshua 1:9).

So what are you waiting for? Start looking for a job today! Then make your first $5,000 faster.

And make your parents proud of you. :)

Don't waste any more time! Start action now.

Thank you for reading my book.
Lord Jesus blesses you.
Amen.

www.ingramcontent.com/pod-product-compliance
Lightning Source LLC
Chambersburg PA
CBHW020559220526
45463CB00006B/2378